Name _____

grab   people   snake
nice   small   wash

Write

The pets have a car _____ .

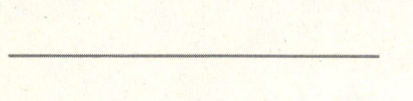

1. A _____ comes.

2. Some _____ come too.

3. The people are _____ to the pets.

4. This is not a _____ job for a dog.

5. But the dog will _____ a rag and wash it.

Directions: Use some words from the story "Pet Wash" to complete these sentences. Read the sentence in the sample. Read the words in bold print at the top of the page. Write the word that belongs in the sentence. Read the sentence again to check your word.

Have pupils draw lines around all the words that name animals. Then have them draw lines under all the words that name things.

"Pet Wash" and "My Very Own Pet," pages 4–15
Vocabulary: key words

1

Draw a line under

Name _____

The friends had a pet wash.
The friends read a book.

1. "What a nice cat," said Rob.
   "That cat is too small," said Rob.

2. The cat had a funny hat.
   The cat ran out.

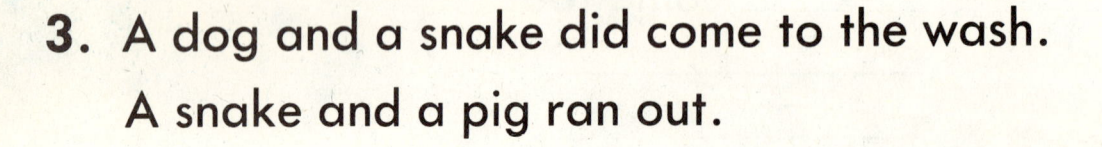

3. A dog and a snake did come to the wash.
   A snake and a pig ran out.

4. Kate said, "Grab that snake!"
   Kate will pat the head of the dog.

5. The pet wash was a people wash.
   A nice horse was at the pet wash.

Directions: This page tells about the story "Pet Wash." Read the two sentences in the sample. Draw a line under the sentence that tells about the story. Do the rest of the page the same way. Look at the story in your books.

Have pupils write a sentence about one of the pets at the pet wash. Then they may draw a picture to go with the sentence.

"Pet Wash" and "My Very Own Pet," pages 4–15
Selection Comprehension: plot

Write   Name _____

It is nice to be at the blue _____ .

land   pond

1. Meg can play in the _____ .

stand   sand

2. Meg can do a hand _____ .

send   stand

3. The _____ is warm at the pond.

band   wind

4. Meg will _____ on her toes now.

send   land

Directions: Some words end with the consonant sounds of **nd**, as in **band**. Read the sentence in the sample. Read the two words in bold print. They both end with the **nd** sound. Write the word that belongs in the sentence. Read the sentence again to check your word.

Have pupils use words that end in **nd** in the sentences.

"Pet Wash" and "My Very Own Pet," pages 4–15
Decoding: nd (hand)

3

Write   Name _____

pig   peg

1. pin   pan

2. wig   wag

3. bug   big

4. not   nut

5. ten   tan

6. dog   dig

7. met   mat

8. fan   fin

Directions: Some words have short vowel sounds: **a** as in **cat**, **e** as in **ten**, **i** as in **pig**, **o** as in **top**, and **u** as in **bug**. Look at the sample. Say the name of the picture. Read the two words in bold print. Write the word that names the picture. Do the rest of the page the same way.

Have pupils add different vowels to finish words: **c–p, h–t, t–p**. Have them write the words they make.

"Pet Wash" and "My Very Own Pet," pages 4–15
Decoding: short vowels a, e, i, o, u

Name _____

Rex said, "Mom, will you dance with me?"

"I can not dance with you now," said Mom.

"Who will dance with me?" Rex said.

"I will," said the fox.

Write

Mom did not dance. Rex was _____ .

nice   sad

1. Rex will _____ with the fox.

run   dance

2. The fox is _____ .

nice   bad

Directions: Characters in stories may be people or animals. Stories tell how characters look, feel, and act. Read the story about Rex. Read the sentence in the sample. Read the two words in bold print. Write the word in the sentence. Do the rest of the page the same way.

Have pupils suggest a different ending to the story. What might have happened if Rex had not found anyone to dance with him?

"Pet Wash" and "My Very Own Pet," pages 4–15
Comprehension: character traits

Fill in the circle

Name _____

The dogs have a new ___.
○ help   ○ house   ○ how

1. The house is for 2 ___ of dogs.
   ○ kinds   ○ kids   ○ know

2. ___ dogs can be big or small.
   ○ This   ○ That   ○ These

3. There are ___ kinds of dogs.
   ○ most   ○ many   ○ may

4. The dogs are ___ by the house.
   ○ there   ○ these   ○ then

5. ___ dogs will fit in the house?
   ○ Where   ○ Which   ○ Who

Directions: Use some words from the story "All Kinds of Pets" to complete these sentences. Read the sentence in the sample. Read the three words in bold print. Fill in the circle beside the word that belongs in the sentence. Read the sentence again to check your word.

Have pupils write their answer to the question at the end of the story.

"All Kinds of Pets," pages 16–19
Vocabulary: key words

© D.C. Heath and Company

Name _____

	Big	Small	In	Out
Check 🐕				
1. 🐴				
2. 🐦				
3. 🦆				
4. 🐰				
5. 🐑				

Directions: This page tells about the story "All Kinds of Pets." Look at the sample. Read the words at the top. They tell about pets. Some pets are big; others are small. Some pets stay in the house; others stay out of the house. Look at the picture in the sample. Put a check in all the boxes that tell about this pet. Do the rest of the page the same way. Look at the story in your books.

Have pupils decide which pet they would most like to have. Have them draw a picture of themselves and that pet, showing what they would do together.

"All Kinds of Pets," pages 16–19
Selection Comprehension: details

© D.C. Heath and Company

Write

Name _____

Is this a big knot? _____

Did he sit on a rock? _____

1. Did she knit it? _____

2. Did he put on a sock? _____

3. Will she knock? _____

4. Can the bird pick up a log? _____

Directions: Some words end with the consonant **ck** sound, as in **back**. Some words begin with the consonant **kn** sound, as in **know**. Each question on this page has a word with **ck** or **kn**. Look at the first picture in the sample. Read the question about the picture. Write **yes** or **no** to answer the question. Do the rest of the page the same way.

Have pupils use the letters **ck** and **kn** to complete these words: **si–, pa–, bri–; –ow, –ee, –ife.**

8 "All Kinds of Pets," pages 16–19
Decoding: ck (duck), kn (knife)

Cross out

Name _____

1.

2.

3.

4.

Directions: Some animals are alike and some are different. For example, a kitten and a hamster are small, but a horse and an elephant are big. Look at the sample. Think about which animals are alike and which are different. Then put an **x** on the picture of the animal that does not belong with the others. Do the rest of the page the same way.

Have pupils tell why the animals in each row are the same or different.

"All Kinds of Pets," pages 16–19
Vocabulary: classification

9

Fill in the circle   Name _____

Many people like hats. Hats help people stay warm. Hats help people look nice.

What is the story about?
○ Hats Can Help You Stay Warm
○ Why People Like Hats

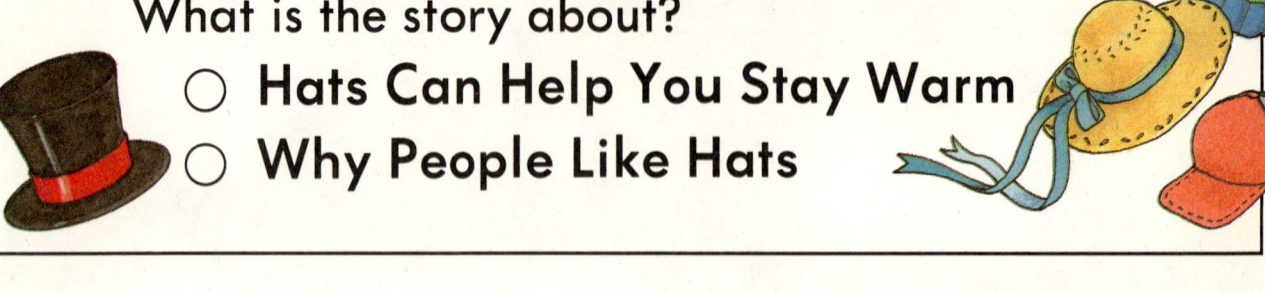

1. You can help at home. You can make a cake. You can bring in the paper.

    What is the story about?
    ○ How You Can Help at Home
    ○ What People Do at Home

2. Beth has many balloons. She has big and small balloons. Some balloons look like a duck and a pig.

    What is the story about?
    ○ A Duck and A Pig
    ○ Lots of Balloons

Directions: The main idea of a story is the most important thing it tells. Sometimes a title tells what the story is about. Read the story in the sample. Read the titles. Fill in the circle next to the title that tells what the story is about. Do the rest of the page the same way.

Have pupils choose one of the stories and write a different title for it. Have pupils share their titles and see if each one fits the story.

"All Kinds of Pets," pages 16–19
Comprehension: main idea

Name _____

asked   does   play   star
boy   name   Shall

Write

Hello! My _____ is Max.

My class will put on a _____ .

Oh _____ ! Now I can be a _____ !

My class _____ me to be the pig.

The pig _____ not do much. But he is big!

_____ I be the pig?

Directions: Use some words from the story "The Play" to complete these sentences. Read the sentence in the sample. Read the words in bold print at the top of the page. Write the word that belongs in the sentence. Read the sentence again to check your word.

Have pupils answer the question at the end of the story and discuss their reasons.

"The Play," pages 20–25
Vocabulary: key words

Name _____

Number

| 1 | Mrs. Fine said, "Class, let's put on a play." |

| ☐ | Mrs. Fine said, "What will I do?" |

| 5 | The class put on a new play, *Seven Snow Whites and the Dwarf*. |

| ☐ | Many people in the class want to be Snow White. |

| ☐ | Max wants to be the dwarf in the play. |

Directions: This page tells about the story "The Play." Read the sentence in the sample. This is what happened first in the story. Trace the **1** in the box. Now read the other sentences. Number them **2, 3, 4** in order to show what happened in the story. Look at the story in your books.

Have pupils write a sentence that tells what they think happened when the play was over and put a **6** in front of it.

12   "The Play," pages 20–25
Selection Comprehension: sequence

Draw a line under

Name _____

See the hot dogs on the green.
See the hot dogs on the grill.

1.

This snack is on a snap.
This snack is good to eat.

2.

I play in the grass.
I play in the shop.

3.

A plum is on the dish.
A plum will eat my snake.

Directions: Some words begin with the consonant sounds of **pl** as in **plan**, **sn** as in **snail**, and **gr** as in **grin**. Look at the picture in the sample. Read the sentences. Draw a line under the sentences that tells about the picture. Read both sentences again to check your work. Do the rest of the page the same way.

Have pupils use their books to find and list words beginning with pl, sn, and gr.

"The Play," pages 20–25
Decoding: pl (plant), sn (snake), gr (green)

13

Name _____

	It Is What You Eat	It Can Sleep	It Is in the House	It Is for Your Hands
Check (mittens)				
1. (birdcage)				
2. (apple)				
3. (stove)				
4. (ring)				
5. (cherries)				

Directions: The chart on this page shows how some things are alike and how they are different. Read the categories across the top. Look at the first picture. Put a check in each box that tells about the picture. Do the rest of the page the same way.

Have pupils name something else that belongs in each group on this page and draw a picture. Then have pupils share pictures and identify categories.

"The Play," pages 20–25
Vocabulary: classification

© D.C. Heath and Company

Draw a line under

Name _____

Jim has a pet rabbit.
The rabbit reads funny books.

1. The cat said, "Hello, you are my friend."
   Jan said, "Hello, you are my friend."

2. Tom and his dog can make a cake.
   Tom and his dad can make a cake.

3. Some birds are blue and red.
   A red bird can go to the stars.

4. A cow can sing and dance.
   A cow can stand and eat.

5. This is a fine, fat frog.
   The frog will dance for you.

Directions: Some stories are about things that could really happen. Other stories are make-believe. Read the sentences in the sample. Draw a line under the sentence that could **not** really happen. Do the rest of the page the same way.

Have pupils change the sentences they underlined to tell something that could really happen.

"The Play," pages 20–25
Comprehension: reality–fantasy

Name _____

Write

cook   Kate's   pizza
cooking   lunch   soon

I like to _____ good things.

1. I will make a big pizza for _____ .

2. I will make the big _____ for Kate.

3. _____ pizza is too hot now.

4. But _____ she can eat it.

5. I like _____ for Kate!

Directions: Use some words from the story "Lunch at Kate's" to complete these sentences. Read the sentence in the sample. Read the words in bold print at the top of the page. Write the word that belongs in the sentence. Read the sentence again to check your word.

Have pupils draw a circle around every word that has something to do with food.

16   "Lunch at Kate's," pages 26–32
Vocabulary: key words

© D.C. Heath and Company

Name _____

Number

_1_ Kate asks Kim to come for lunch.

_5_ The friends have pizza for lunch.

___ Kate's mom has to go out.

___ Kate asks Rob and Max too.

___ Kim asks Mom if she can go.

Directions: This page tells about the story "Lunch at Kate's." Read the sentence in the sample. This happened first in the story. Trace the **1** on the line. Now read the rest of the sentences. Number them **2, 3, 4** to tell what happened in the story. Look at the story in your books.

Have pupils write a sentence telling what they like to eat when they invite a friend to lunch. They can draw a picture to go with the sentence.

"Lunch at Kate's," pages 26–32
Selection Comprehension: sequence

Write Name _____

Don said, "Dad will get some _____."

                                      chicks   chat

1. The chicks do not cost _____.

                     such   much

2. I will help Dad _____ them.

                 check   chin

3. The chicks must not get a _____.

                     such   chill

4. We will put them in a _____ to stay warm.

                     chest   check

Directions: Some words have the consonant **ch** sound, as in **chair** and **beach.** Read the sentence in the sample. Read the two words in bold print. Write the word that belongs in the sentence. Read the sentence again to check your word.

Have pupils look through magazines to find pictures of things that begin with **ch** and have the same beginning sound as **church.** Pupils can make a **ch** bulletin board or chart.

18   "Lunch at Kate's," pages 26–32
Decoding: <u>ch</u> (church)

Write Name _____

We are _____ .
fished   fishing

1. I am _____ this lunch.
cooked   cooking

2. My mom is _____ me.
helped   helping

3. I _____ Bill to have lunch.
asked   asking

Directions: Sometimes words have **ed** or **ing** at the end. Look at the picture in the sample. Read the sentence and the words in bold print. Write the word that belongs in the sentence. Read the sentence again to check your word.

Have pupils write their own sentences using one of these word pairs: **played/playing, washed/washing, looked/looking.**

"Lunch at Kate's," pages 26–32
Decoding: inflections **-ed, -ing**

19

Write

Name _____

The cat has a hat.

_____

It is the _____ hat.

---

1. The hen has a pen.

   _____

   It is the _____ pen.

---

2. The fox has a box.

   _____

   It is the _____ box.

---

3. The pig has a wig.

   _____

   It is the _____ wig.

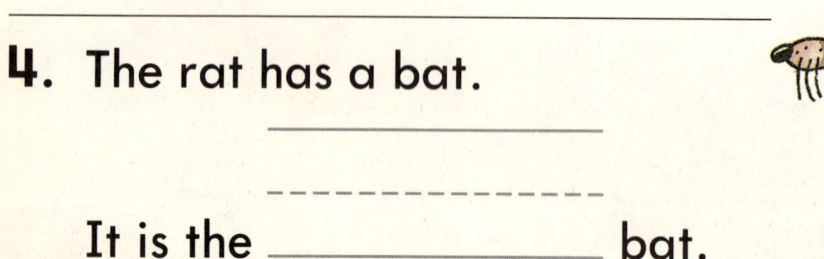

---

4. The rat has a bat.

   _____

   It is the _____ bat.

Directions: An **apostrophe** and **s** are added to show that something belongs to someone. Look at the sample and read the first sentence. Think about who owns something. Write the word that belongs in the second sentence. Do the rest of the page the same way.

Have pupils write these pairs of sentences, filling in the blanks: **Peg has a** _____. **It is** _____ _____. **Bob has a** _____. **It is** _____ _____.

"Lunch at Kate's," pages 26–32
Decoding: possessives -'s

20

© D.C. Heath and Company

Number

Name _____

	She sees a puppy at a shop.	She takes the puppy home.

He is ready to go out.		He plays in the snow.

	The boy is eating.	The boy can make things to eat.

She gets a stamp.	She puts "Hello, Max" on some paper.	

Directions: As you read a story think about the order in which things happen. Look at the picture and the sentences in the sample. Number them **1, 2, 3** to show the order of what happens. Do the rest of the page the same way.

Have pupils name three things they do when they are getting ready to go to bed. Ask them to think of what they do first, second, and third and draw pictures showing the order.

"Lunch at Kate's," pages 26–32
Comprehension: sequence

Fill in the circle

Name _____

We are ____ to make pizza.
○ going   ○ go   ○ got

1. The ____ will help.
   ○ thank   ○ teacher   ○ them

2. She will tell us ____ we do a good job.
   ○ it   ○ if   ○ of

3. Do steps 4, 5, and 6 ____ the pizza will not be good.
   ○ or   ○ off   ○ out

4. Cook it till it is ____.
   ○ too   ○ not   ○ hot

5. Take it out ____ the bell rings.
   ○ who   ○ when   ○ which

6. Then eat ____!
   ○ snake   ○ going   ○ everything

Directions: Use some words from the story "Lunch With Your Friends" to complete these sentences. Read the sentence in the sample. Read the three words in bold print. Fill in the circle beside the word that belongs in the sentence. Read the sentence again to check your word.

Make a recipe for pizza with the class. Have the pupils suggest the steps in the process. Write the steps on the board. Have pupils write the recipe and take it home.

"Lunch With Your Friends," pages 33–37
Vocabulary: key words

© D.C. Heath and Company

Write

Name _____

Can friends help make pizza? _____

1. Will you ask a friend to help? _____

2. Will you wash your hands? _____

3. Will you get everything ready? _____

4. Will you put a balloon on your pizza? _____

5. Will you eat the pizza if it is too hot? _____

Directions: This page is about the story "Lunch With Your Friends." Read the question in the sample and think about the story. Write **yes** or **no** to answer the question. Do the rest of the page the same way. Look at the story in your books.

Have pupils discuss what they can make for lunch. Have them draw a picture showing how they make that food and write this sentence under the picture: **I can make _____ for lunch.**

"Lunch With Your Friends," pages 33–37
Selection Comprehension: details

23

Write   Name _____

She will run and play.

She will _____ too.

stick   kick

1.  He is not well.

He is _____ .

sock   sick

2.  Can she go in?

She will _____ .

knit   knock

3. 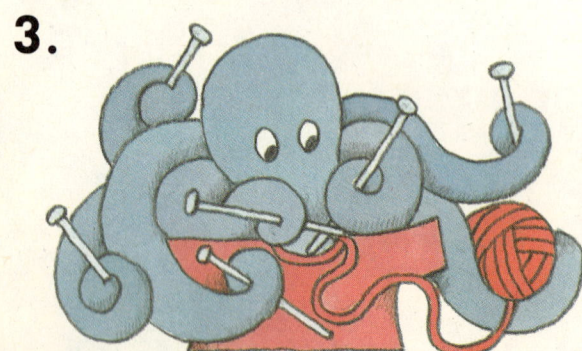 He will make a hat for you.

He will _____ it.

knot   knit

Directions: Some words have the consonant sound of **kn** as in **knob** or **ck** as in **duck**. Look at the picture in the sample. Read the sentences and the words in bold print. Write the word that belongs in the sentence. Read the sentence again to check your word.

Have pupils choose a **ck** word they did not write. Write a sentence using that word.

24   "Lunch With Your Friends," pages 33–37
Decoding: **ck** (duck), **kn** (knife)

Draw a line around   Name _____

snake

1. cake

2. Kate

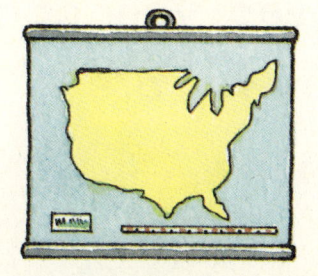

3. game

4. made

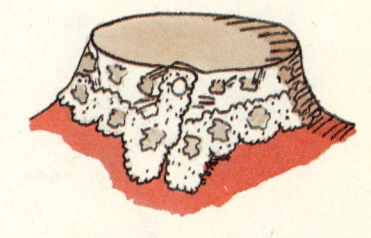

Directions: Some words have a long **a** vowel sound, as in **tape.** Read the word in the sample. Look at the pictures in the row. Draw a line around the pictures whose names have the long **a** sound. There may be more than one picture in each row with the long **a** vowel sound.

Have pupils write the word that names each picture they circled on the page.

"Lunch With Your Friends," pages 33–37
Decoding: a (cake)

25

Fill in the circle

Name _____

You can do many things with paper.

You can cut it to make a hat. You can make a paper book.

What is the story about?
○ Things to Make with Hats
○ Things to Make with Paper

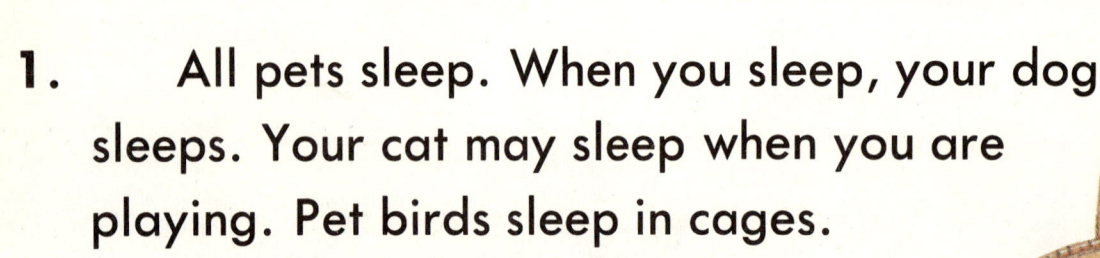

1. All pets sleep. When you sleep, your dog sleeps. Your cat may sleep when you are playing. Pet birds sleep in cages.

   What is the story about?
   ○ Sleep for Pets
   ○ Sleeping in a Cage

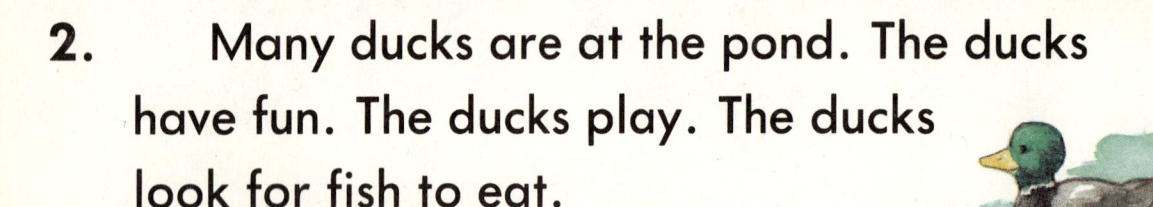

2. Many ducks are at the pond. The ducks have fun. The ducks play. The ducks look for fish to eat.

   What is the story about?
   ○ Fish for Ducks
   ○ Ducks at the Pond

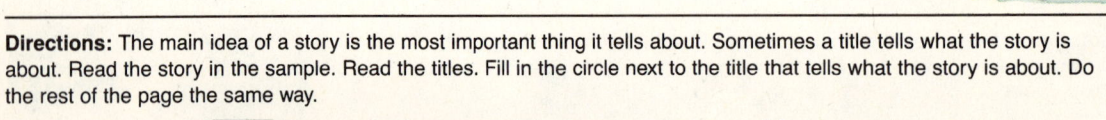

Directions: The main idea of a story is the most important thing it tells about. Sometimes a title tells what the story is about. Read the story in the sample. Read the titles. Fill in the circle next to the title that tells what the story is about. Do the rest of the page the same way.

Have pupils choose one of the titles they did not use. Have them tell a round-robin story that might have that title, each pupil adding one sentence.

"Lunch With Your Friends," pages 33–37
Comprehension: main idea

Name _____

Write green   mix   paint   stop   today

Carlos wanted to _____ the house.

"I will get paint _____," said Carlos.

"Can we _____ for pizza?" said Max.

"I just want _____ paint," said Carlos.

"You can _____ blue paint and yellow paint," said Max.

"Good!" said Carlos. "Then we will get some pizza."

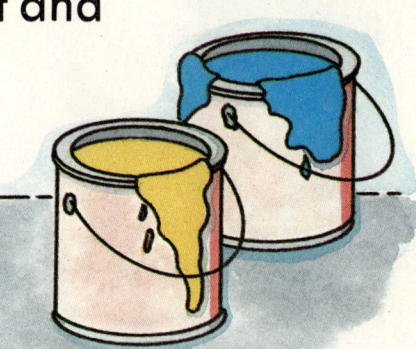

Directions: Use some words from the story "Look Out!" to complete these sentences. Read the sentence in the sample. Read the words in bold print at the top of the page. Write the word that belongs in the sentence. Read the sentence again to check your word.

Have pupils write one sentence using the words **green** and **paint**. They can draw a picture to go with their sentence.

"Look Out!" pages 38–42
Vocabulary: key words

27

Draw a line to

Name _____

Kate.   . said, "Today we are
                           all going to paint."

Mrs. Fine.   . said, "We can mix
                           blue and yellow paint."

1. Carlos   .   . said, "We ran out
                           of green paint."

2. Mrs. Fine .   . got out
                           some paper.

3. Meg .   . spilled
                           the paint.

4. The cat   . said, "Look what the
   and dog .   dog and cat did!"

Directions: This page is about the story "Look Out!" Look at the sample and read the names of the characters. Then read the sentences that tell about the characters. Draw a line from the characters' names to the words that tell what they did in the story. Do the rest of the page the same way. Look at the story in your books.

Have pupils think about how the dog and cat made a painting. Ask what they think the painting looked like. Have them write two sentences about the painting and draw a picture to go with them.

28   "Look Out!" pages 38–42
Selection Comprehension: character traits/plot

© D.C. Heath and Company

Write

Name _____

You can use this.

_____

It is a _____ .

dime   dive

1. We have bikes.

_____

We will go for a _____ .

ripe   ride

2. She got a fish.

_____

The fish is _____ to eat.

file   fine

3. The men do a job.

_____

The _____ is very big.

pipe   pile

Directions: Some words have the long **i** vowel sound, as in **ride**. Look at the sample. The picture names a long **i** word. Read the sentences and the words in bold print. Write the word that belongs in the sentence. Read the sentence again to check your word.

Have pupils give oral sentences using the words that were not answers.

"Look Out!" pages 38–42
Decoding: i (kite)

Draw a line around

Name _____

This bird is a blue jay.
yes   no

1.  He will go on a train.
yes   no

2.  She will pay.
yes   no

3.  The cows are eating hay.
yes   no

4.  We play in the rain.
yes   no

5.  She has a gray pail.
yes   no

Directions: Some words have the long **a** vowel sound. Each sentence on the page has a word with the long **a** vowel sound spelled **ai** as in **tail** or **ay** as in **stay**. Look at the picture in the sample. Read the sentence. Draw a line around **yes** or **no** to answer the question. Do the rest of the page the same way.

Have pupils fill in the blanks to make words that are not on this page: _____ **ay**, _____ **ail**. Have pupils share their words to see how many different words they have written.

"Look Out!" pages 38–42
Decoding: <u>ai</u> (train), <u>ay</u> (play)

© D.C. Heath and Company

Draw a line around   Name _____

She has no balloon.   She wants a balloon.

1. Mom fixed Kate's cut hand. Then she fixed the cake.

2. He went on a hike.   A snake bit him.

3. He is a teacher.   His class is going on a trip.

Directions: Sometimes you can tell what will happen next in a story. Read the two sentences in the sample. Look at the two pictures. Think about what will happen next. Draw a line around the picture that shows what will probably happen next. Do the rest of the page the same way.

Have pupils write a sentence and give it to a classmate to tell what might happen next.

"Look Out!" pages 38–42
Comprehension: predict outcomes

31

Draw a line under

Name _____

Meg got the blue paint.

1. The pizza is ready.
2. My dad is a good cook too!
3. Max wants to be a dwarf.
4. Some pets are small.
5. My friend can wash a pet.

Write

People and Things

Directions: Some words name people, places, or things. A sentence tells about a person, place or thing. At the top of the page, draw a line under the person or thing each sentence is about. At the bottom of the page, write the names of the people or things you would like to write about. Save your notes in your folder.

Draw a picture of one of the people or things you want to write about.

"Look Out!" pages 38–42
Language: writing process (prewriting)

© D.C. Heath and Company

Name _____

Write   grandma   hair   his   lives   where

Carlos _____ with his mom.

His _____ and his Uncle Louie live on the same block. Uncle Louie has a bear.

Carlos likes to go to _____ grandma's house. He likes the way she cuts his _____ .

But Carlos likes the house _____ he lives the best.

Directions: Use some words from the story "Uncle Louie" to complete these sentences. Read the sentence in the sample. Read the words in bold print at the top of the page. Write the word that belongs in the sentence. Read the sentence again to check your word.

Have pupils draw a line around all the words that name people on this page.

"Uncle Louie," pages 43–47
Vocabulary: key words

33

Write   Name _____

Does Carlos tell his friends about Uncle Louie?

1. Do his friends know Uncle Louie?

2. Does Uncle Louie have a lot of hair?

3. Does Uncle Louie like to play with his bear?

4. Does Uncle Louie live with Carlos's grandma?

5. Does Uncle Louie read funny books?

Directions: This page asks questions about the story "Uncle Louie." Read the question in the sample and think about the story. Write **yes** or **no** to answer the question. Do the rest of the page the same way. Look at the story in your books.

Have pupils discuss what they think Carlos's friends said when they saw Uncle Louie.

34   "Uncle Louie," pages 43–47
Selection Comprehension: character traits

Name _____

Write   aren't   doesn't   isn't
             can't   hasn't

She <u>is not</u> running.

She _____ running.

1. She <u>can not</u> skate.

   She _____ skate.

2. He <u>does not</u> like to slide.

   He _____ like to slide.

3. He <u>has not</u> played with his bat.

   He _____ played with his bat.

4. We <u>are not</u> doing a thing.

   We _____ doing a thing.

Directions: This page gives practice in contractions. Read the sentences in the sample. Read the words in bold print at the top of the page. Write the contraction that stands for the underlined words. Read the sentence again to check your word.

Have pupils ask a question using two words that can be answered using a contraction at the top of the page. Other pupils respond to the question.

"Uncle Louie," pages 43–47
Decoding: contraction (verb + <u>not</u>)

35

Draw a line around

Name _____

Where **Who**

Directions: This page is about people, places, and things that go together. Look at the pictures in the first box of the sample. They are all things that go together. The second box shows places. Draw a line around the place where the things in the first picture belong. The last box shows people. Draw a line around the person who belongs in the first two pictures. Do the rest of the page the same way.

Think about a place where you would like to be. Draw a picture of that place. Show some things and people who belong in that place.

"Uncle Louie," pages 43–47
Comprehension: characters / setting

© D.C. Heath and Company

Draw a line under

Name _____

Uncle Louie plays with his bear.

1. They mix blue and yellow paint.
2. Dad cooks good pizza.
3. We ate lots of pizza.
4. My cat sleeps in my house.
5. Grab that snake!

Write

Directions: Some words like **jump** and **throw** tell what a person or thing is doing. A sentence tells about a person or thing and about what the person or thing is doing. Read the sentence in the sample. Draw a line under the word that tells what Uncle Louie is doing. Do the top of the page the same way.

At the bottom of the page, write a sentence telling about something a person or thing does. Begin with a capital letter. End with a period.

Read your sentence to a friend.

"Uncle Louie," pages 43–47
Language: writing process (writing)

37

Name _____

bus   down   off   out   sat   stopped

Write

We went on a _____ ride.

My friends and I _____ down in the back.

The bus went to the top of the hill and back _____ .

Soon the bus _____ .

I looked _____ of the bus at some ducks.

We got _____ the bus. I gave nuts to the ducks. The ducks love nuts.

Directions: Use some words from the story "On the Bus" to complete these sentences. Read the sentence in the sample. Read the words in bold print at the top of the page. Write the word that belongs in the sentence. Read the sentence again to check your word.

Have pupils write this sentence, filling in the blank: **Squirrels love to eat ___ .** They can draw a picture to go with their sentence.

38   "On the Bus" and "The Wheels on the Bus," pages 48–59
Vocabulary: key words

Draw a line under

Name _____

Carlos, Kim, and Max ran to the bus stop.
Carlos, Kim, and Max ran home.

1. Max got on the bus and sat with Kate.
   Max sat in the back of the big bus.

2. Big Ed sat with Kim.
   Big Ed sat with Max.

3. Big Ed said, "Have a nut."
   Big Ed said, "Your hat looks funny."

4. Big Ed and Max ate lunch.
   Big Ed and Max ate nuts.

5. When the bus stops, Max and Big Ed are friends.
   Max helped Big Ed get off the bus.

Directions: This page tells about the story "On the Bus." Read the two sentences in the sample. Think about what happened in the story. Draw a line under the sentence that tells what happened. Do the rest of the page the same way. Look at the story in your books.

Have pupils discuss what they think happened the next time Max saw Big Ed. Have pupils write a short conversation between them. Remind them to use quotation marks.

"On the Bus" and "The Wheels on the Bus," pages 48–59
Selection Comprehension: plot

Name _____

Write

be   by   go   me   so   try   Why

I want to _____ to my grandma's house.

Will you come with _____ ?

We can go _____ bus.

_____ do you want to go there?

My grandma is _____ nice. She will take us to the pond. We can _____ to get a frog.

A frog will _____ a good pet.

Directions: Practice using words that have a long vowel sound at the end. Read the sentence in the sample. Read the words in bold print at the top of the page. Write the word that belongs in the sentence. Read the sentence again to check your word.

Have pupils write one sentence using these words: **we, sky, go.** Have pupils compare their sentences to see how many different ways they have used the words.

40   "On the Bus" and "The Wheels on the Bus," pages 48–59
Decoding: syllable patterns (CV)

Write

Name _____

The cows are _____.

run + ing

1. The fox is _____.

sit + ing

2. The pig is _____.

hop + ing

3. The snail is _____.

win + ing

4. The alligator is _____.

nap + ing

Directions: When **ing** is added to some words, like **tip** and **grin**, the consonant at the end of the word is doubled before the ending is added. Read the sentence in the sample. Read the word in bold print. Add **ing** to the word and write it in the sentence. Remember to double the final consonant.

Have pupils write sentences using the words **stopping** and **getting**. Draw a line around the root word for each word.

"On the Bus" and "The Wheels on the Bus," pages 48–59
Decoding: spelling changes (doubled consonant before ending)

Name _____

Pat loved his new red hat. He played in it. He went to sleep in it too. But when he got up, Pat's hat was not there.

Pat and Mom looked and looked for the hat. But Pat and Mom did not see it. Then Mom said, "Ask Dad."

"Dad!" said Pat. "Do you have my hat?"

"Yes," said Dad. "It helped me stay warm."

Then Pat's hat stayed on his head!

Draw a line under

Why did Pat's mom look and look?
   She wanted to get a hat for Dad.
   She was helping Pat look for his hat.

1. Why didn't Pat get mad at his dad?
   He was glad to get his hat back.
   His dad helped him look for the hat.

2. What is the best name for this story?
   Pat's Hat
   Pat's Mom Has a Hat

Directions: Think about the characters and what they did as you read the story. Read the question in the sample. Draw a line under the correct answer. Do the rest of the page the same way.

Have pupils tell how they know that Pat likes his hat. What are details in the story?

"On the Bus" and "The Wheels on the Bus," pages 48–59
Comprehension: character traits/plot

Name _____

Write

again   school   wished
jumped   tooth

Meg _____ for a tooth to come out.

She wished all day in _____ .

Then she _____ and hopped home.

"Will you look at my _____ ?" Meg asked Mom.

Mom looked. Then she looked _____ . Meg's tooth was out!

Directions: Use some words from the story "Not Yet" to complete these sentences. Read the sentence in the sample. Read the words in the bold print at the top of the page. Write the word that belongs in the sentence. Read the sentence again to check your word.

Have pupils write "I Wish" at the top of their paper. Ask them to write three sentences about their wish.

"Not Yet," pages 60–66
Vocabulary: key words

43

Draw a line to

Name _____

1. •   • Rob ate a lot to make his tooth come out.

2. •   • Meg's tooth came out.

3. •   • Dad said, "Go to sleep. That may help."

4. •   • Mom said, "Go out and play. That may help."

5. •   • Rob fell and his tooth came out.

6. •   • Rob said, "Oh, no! Here we go again."

7. •   • Meg said, "My tooth is out!"

Directions: This page tells about the story "Not Yet." Look the sample and read the numbers and sentences. Draw a line from number 1 to the sentence that tells what happened first in the story. Draw a line from number 2 to the sentence that tells what happened second. Do the rest of the page the same way. Look at the story in your books.

Have pupils write a sentence telling how many teeth they have lost. Ask them to draw a picture of what they were doing when their teeth fell out.

"Not Yet," pages 60–66
Selection Comprehension: sequence

Write   Name _____

We are _____ a cake.
bake + ing

1. She is _____ a dog balloon.
make + ing

2. My friends are _____.
come + ing

3. He is _____ some cake.
take + ing

4. We are all _____ fun.
have + ing

Directions: Some words end with an **e**, like **tape** and **love**. When **ing** is added to these words, the spelling of the root word changes. The final **e** is dropped. Read the sentence in the sample. Read the word in bold print. Add **ing** to the word and write it in the sentence. Remember to drop the final **e** before adding the ending. Read the sentence again to check your word. Do the rest of the page the same way.

Have pupils write a sentence using **live + ing**.

"Not Yet," pages 60–66
Decoding: spelling changes (dropped -e before ending)

45

Write   Name _____

fox
_____

1. bus
_____

2. dish
_____

3. box
_____

4. dress
_____

5. brush
_____

6. lunch
_____

Directions: Sometimes **es** is added to a word to mean more than one. Look at the picture in the sample. Write the word that means more than one. Do the rest of the page the same way.

Have pupils write the plural forms of **wish** and **class**.

46   "Not Yet," pages 60–66
Decoding: inflections -es (noun)

Write   s   ed   ing

Jack is wishing for his tooth to come out.

I am _____ for my tooth to come out.

wish

1. I jumped up and down.

   Jack is _____ too.

   jump

2. I looked at my tooth.

   Jack stops and _____ at his tooth.

   look

3. Jack has waited for the tooth to come out.

   I have _____ too.

   wait

Directions: Sometimes words have **s, ed,** or **ing** on the end. Read the sentences in the sample. Look at the word in bold print. Write the word in the sentence. Add **s, ed,** or **ing.** Read the sentence again.

Have pupils write each word in bold print with the other endings.

"Not Yet," pages 60–66
Decoding: inflections -s, -ed, -ing

47

Fill in the circle

Name _____

"The paint is too thick.
We can not paint," said Len.
"Yes, we can," said Stan.
"I know how."
What will the boys do now?

1. "I have a new pet," said Jill.
"It is very long and very thin."
"Is it a long dog?" asked Tom.
"No," said Jill. "My pet does not have legs."
What pet will Jill show Tom?

2. Dot said, "Do you like the pond?"
"Yes, I do," said Jen.
Dot asked, "Do you like fish?"
"Yes," said Jen.
"Then come with me," Dot said.
What will Dot and Jen do?

Directions: Sometimes you can tell what will happen next in a story. Read the story in the sample. Think about what will happen next. Look at the pictures. Fill in the circle next to the picture that shows what will probably happen next. Do the rest of the page the same way.

Have pupils underline the clues in each story that helped them decide what would happen next.

"Not Yet," pages 60–66
Comprehension: predict outcomes

Name _____

bulbs   grow   They
garden   plant   You'll

Write

Dad and I dug a _____ .

We got some seeds and _____ .

"Shall we _____ the seeds and bulbs here?" asked Dad. "There is nothing here now."

"Yes," I said. "_____ will look nice here. Will they _____ soon?"

"_____ see," said Dad.

Directions: Use some words from the story "The Garden" to complete these sentences. Read the sentence in the sample. Read the words at the top of the page. Write the word that belongs in the sentence. Read the sentence again to check your word.

Have pupils write a sentence about the new plants. Have them use the word **grew** in the sentence.

"The Garden" and "Maytime Magic," pages 67–75
Vocabulary: key words

49

Draw a line under Name _____

Mrs. Fine wanted to plant bulbs.
Mrs. Fine wanted to plant seeds.

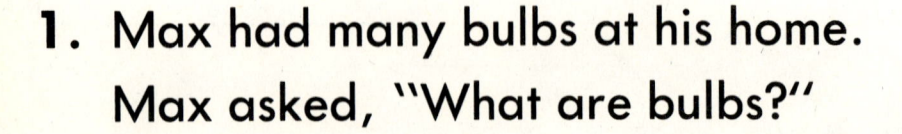

1. Max had many bulbs at his home.
   Max asked, "What are bulbs?"

2. Mrs. Fine said, "Bulbs are like seeds."
   Mrs. Fine said, "The bulbs will be nice."

3. Mrs. Fine planted the bulbs.
   Mrs. Fine and the class planted the bulbs.

4. The bulbs grew in the garden.
   The bulbs grew on a path.

5. When they grew, the plants looked very nice.
   The class did not like the things that grew.

Directions: This page tells about the story "The Garden." Read the two sentences in the sample. Draw a line under the sentence that tells what happened in the story. Do the rest of the page the same way. Look at the story in your books.

Have pupils imagine what the class did with the flowers they grew. Pupils can draw pictures showing their ideas. Then they can compare their different ideas.

"The Garden" and "Maytime Magic," pages 67–75
Selection Comprehension: plot

Draw a line around

Name _____

My grandma likes to zum the day in the garden.
I zum my day with my grandma.
brick   spend   dive

1. Grandma can't weth very well.
   I weth down and put seeds in the garden.
   bend   melt   wait

2. Grandma does not like glits in the garden.
   I pick up the glits and toss them out.
   bulbs   seeds   rocks

3. When it slonks, we go inside.
   The seeds get wet when it slonks.
   lands   rains   digs

4. Grandma says, "Do not hoth the small green plants."
   "Wait and hoth them when they are big."
   pick   have   help

Directions: Read the sentences in the sample. The underlined word is a nonsense word. It stands for a real word. Read the words in bold print. Draw a line around the word that belongs in both of the sentences in place of the nonsense word. Read the sentences again with your word.

Have pupils make up two sentences with the same nonsense word in each one. Have pupils share their sentences orally and have classmates decide the real word.

"The Garden" and "Maytime Magic," pages 67–75
Decoding: context clues

Fill in the circle

Name _____

Jan and Fran planted some seeds.
They take care of the garden.
- ○ Seeds can not grow.
- ○ New plants will grow.

1. Dad gets some paint. He gets a brush.
   - ○ Dad will paint the garden.
   - ○ Dad will paint his house.

2. May wants a pet. Mom doesn't like birds. Dad doesn't like cats. May goes to a pet shop.
   - ○ May will get a cat.
   - ○ May will get a fish.

3. Grandma gets some cans. She gets the dog's dish and the cat's dish. Then she gets the dog and the cat.
   - ○ Grandma will run with the dog and cat.
   - ○ The dog and cat will eat.

Directions: Sometimes you can tell what will happen next in a story. Read the story in the sample. Read the sentences. Fill in the circle beside the sentence that tells what will probably happen next. Do the rest of the page the same way.

Have pupils tell what happened when May got home with her new pet.

"The Garden" and "Maytime Magic," pages 67–75
Comprehension: predict outcomes

Draw a line around

Name _____

We know how to plant bulbs.

1. You plant bulbs in your garden.
2. My garden.
3. You wait and wait.
4. Nothing green garden.
5. The bulbs grow when it gets warm.

Write

Directions: A complete sentence tells about a person or thing and about what the person or thing is doing. Read the words in the sample. If they make a sentence, draw a line around the words. If they don't make a sentence, leave it blank. Do the top of the page the same way.

At the bottom of the page, copy only the complete sentences from the top of the page. Write neatly. Begin each sentence with a capital letter and end with a period.

Give your sentences to a friend to read.

"The Garden" and "Maytime Magic," pages 67–75
Language: writing process (editing, postwriting)

Name _____

Write   from   little   plants   tell   up

Kate put seeds and bulbs in the garden.

She likes to see new _____ grow.

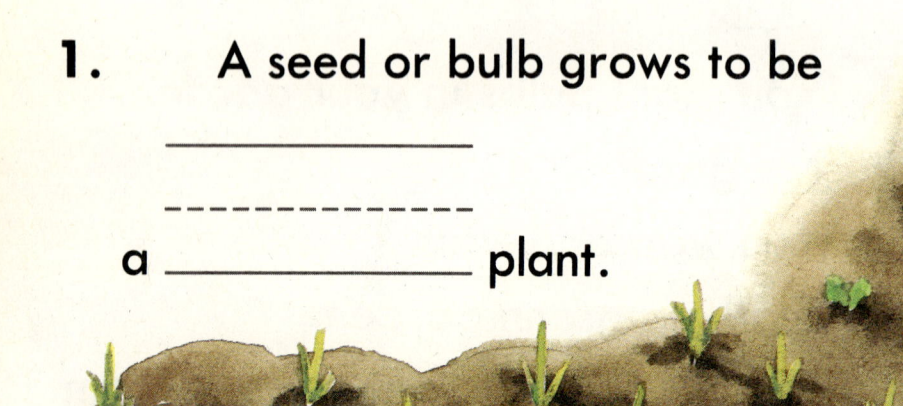

1. A seed or bulb grows to be _____

   a _____ plant.

2. Kate sees the plants come _____ .

   Soon Kate picks them _____ the garden.

   She will _____ Grandma about them.

Directions: Use some words from the story "Seeds and Bulbs" to complete these sentences. Look at the sample and read the sentences. Read the words in bold print at the top of the page. Write the word that belongs in the sentence. Read the sentence again to check your word.

Have pupils look through a seed catalog to find plants that grow from seeds and plants that grow from bulbs.

"Seeds and Bulbs," pages 76–79
Vocabulary: key words

Write

Name _____

Do some plants grow from bulbs? _____

1. Are all bulbs big? _____

2. Are all seeds little? _____

3. Can a big plant grow from a little seed? _____

4. Do plants need many things to grow? _____

5. Does everything on a plant grow up? _____

Directions: This page asks questions about the story "Seeds and Bulbs." Read the question in the sample. Think about the story. Write **yes** or **no** to answer the question. Do the rest of the page the same way. Look at the story in your books.

Have pupils find out what the parts of a plant are called. Then they can draw a picture and label parts such as root, stem, leaf, and flower.

"Seeds and Bulbs," pages 76–79
Selection Comprehension: details

55

Draw a line around Name _____

> There is a drish in my garden.
> The birds sit on the drish and sing.
> brick   dog   gate

1. Some plants are big and rafe.
   They are rafe like the sun.
   yellow   blue   mad

2. The plants all have suts.
   Some suts are thin and green.
   sand   sun   stems

3. The sun pligs on nice days.
   It pligs on a plant and makes it grow.
   rains   shines   sings

4. A crig is a tall cup.
   You can put plants in a crig.
   vase   kite   chop

Directions: Read the sentences in the sample. The underlined word is a nonsense word. It stands for a real word. Read the words in bold print. One word will fit in both sentences in place of the nonsense word. Draw a line around the word that belongs in both sentences. Read the sentences again with your word.

Have pupils use two of the words they chose in new sentences.

"Seeds and Bulbs," pages 76–79
Decoding: context clues

Draw a line under

Name _____

You did a <u>nice</u> job.
  new   funny   good

1. The cat likes to <u>nap</u> in the sun.
    sit   sleep   run

2. He will <u>grab</u> the snake.
    get   see   read

3. You must <u>wait</u> here.
    go   stay   cook

4. I am <u>fine</u> today.
    sick   well   sad

5. I want a <u>little</u> dog.
    small   big   new

Directions: Some words have meanings that are the same or almost the same as other words. Read the sentence in the sample. Read the words in bold print. Draw a line under the word that means the same or almost the same as the underlined word.

Have pupils think of other words and their synonyms.

"Seeds and Bulbs," pages 76–79
Vocabulary: synonyms

Draw a line around

Name _____

We see a big yellow bus. It has a blue flag.

1. We see a brown and white horse.
   It is running.

2. We see a green frog and red bugs sitting on a big rock.

3. We see a big white duck and five little ducks in a pond.

Directions: These sentences tell about real things. Read the sentence in the sample. Think about the facts the sentence tells you. Look at the pictures. Draw a line around the picture that shows what the sentence tells about.

Have pupils draw a picture of an animal and write a sentence about it on another piece of paper. Have other pupils match the pictures and the sentences.

"Seeds and Bulbs," pages 76–79
Comprehension: main idea/details

© D.C. Heath and Company

Name _____

bugs   get   rocks
Everyone   liked   show

Write

"It's time for the _____," said Rob.

_____ will have fun.

Rob has a box with bugs and _____ in it.

The little _____ live in the rocks.

"I _____ it—bug houses!" said Kate.

We all _____ Rob's Show and Tell.

Directions: Use some words from the story "Show and Tell" to complete these sentences. Read the sentence in the sample. Read the words in bold print at the top of the page. Write the word that belongs in the sentence. Read the sentence again to check your word.

Have pupils finish these sentences: **Today I liked** _____ . **I showed** _____ .

"Show and Tell," pages 90–96
Vocabulary: key words

59

Name _____

___ Mrs. Fine said it was time for Show and Tell.

___ 1. Meg showed a book at Show and Tell.

___ 2. Some of the class didn't like the book.

___ 3. Max showed a hat.

___ 4. Kate showed some rocks.

___ 5. Everyone liked Rob's bugs.

___ 6. Kim showed many friends.

Directions: This page tells about the story "Show and Tell." Look at the picture and read the sentence in the sample. If the sentence tells something that happened in the story, put a check on the line. If the sentence does not tell what happened in the story, leave the line blank. Do the rest of the page the same way. Look at the story in your books.

Have pupils draw a picture of something they would like to show during Show and Tell and write one thing they would tell about it.

"Show and Tell," pages 90–96
Selection Comprehension: plot

Name _____

| bag | bug | fox | mop | pen |
| box | cat | hen | pan | pig |

Write

This _____ has a _____ .

1. This _____ has a _____ .

2. This _____ has a _____ .

3. This _____ has a _____ .

4. This _____ has a _____ .

Directions: Some words have short vowel sounds: **a** as in **cat**, **e** as in **ten**, **i** as in **pig**, **o** as in **pot**, or **u** as in **bug**. Read the words at the top of the page. Look at the picture in the sample. Read the sentence. Write the words that belong in the sentence. Read the sentence again to check your words.

Have pupils draw a picture to go with this sentence. **Ten men sat on a big red bug.** Then have them write the sentence under the picture.

"Show and Tell," pages 90–96
Decoding: short vowels a, e, i, o, u

61

© D.C. Heath and Company

Draw a line under

Name _____

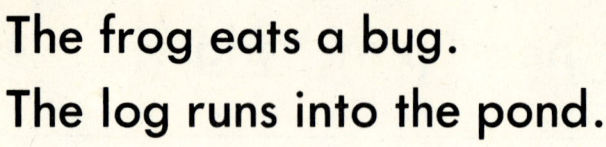

The frog eats a bug.
The log runs into the pond.

1. The frog smiles and waves his hand.

2. "Hello, how are you?" the bugs ask the man.

3. The frog jumps into the pond.

4. The man looks at the duck.

5. The duck says, "Quack, quack."

6. The duck drives a big bus.

7. The man says, "Everything looks so nice here."

8. The plants say, "We want you to stay."

Directions: Some stories tell about things that could really happen. Other stories tell about make-believe things. Read the sentences in the sample. Draw a line under the sentence that tells about something that could **not** really happen. Do the rest of the page the same way.

Have pupils change the underlined sentences to tell something that could really happen.

"Show and Tell," pages 90–96
Comprehension: reality–fantasy

62

© D.C. Heath and Company

Max the Cook

Max the Fox liked to cook.
He made green pizza and rock cake.

"Max is not a good cook," said his friends Kate the Cow and Ed the Pig.

© D.C. Heath and Company

The next day Kate and Ed went to Max's house.

"Lunch is ready," said Max.
"The book helped me cook.
I made rock pizza and green cake!"

"Oh!" said Kate and Ed.

Max asked Kate and Ed to lunch.
They did not want to go.
"Max is not a good cook," said Ed.
"I know what we can do," said Kate.
"We can give Max a book to help him cook."

Kate and Ed went to Max's house.
"We have a book for you," said Kate.
"Oh good!" said Max.